EUCHARISTIC ADORATION

Reflections in the Franciscan Tradition

FRANCISCAN SISTERS OF
PERPETUAL ADORATION

ST. ANTHONY MESSENGER PRESS
Cincinnati, Ohio

RESCRIPT

In accord with the Code of Canon Law, I hereby grant my permission to publish *Eucharistic Adoration: Reflections in the Franciscan Tradition* by the Franciscan Sisters of Perpetual Adoration.

Most Reverend Joseph Binzer
Vicar General and Auxiliary Bishop
of the Archdiocese of Cincinnati
Cincinnati, Ohio
December 14, 2011

The permission to publish is a declaration that a book or pamphlet is considered to be free from doctrinal or moral error. It is not implied that those who have granted the permission to publish agree with the contents, opinions or statements expressed.

Excerpts from *Clare of Assisi: Early Documents* used with permission by the Franciscan Institute, St. Bonaventure, New York. All rights reserved.

Scripture passages have been taken from *New Revised Standard Version Bible,* copyright ©1989 by the Division of Christian Education of the National Council of the Churches of Christ in the U.S.A., and used by permission. All rights reserved.

Cover and book design by Mark Sullivan
Cover image copyright © fotolia | zatletic

LIBRARY OF CONGRESS CATALOGING-IN-PUBLICATION DATA
Eucharistic adoration : reflections in the Franciscan tradition / Franciscan Sisters of Perpetual Adoration.
        p. cm.
    Includes bibliographical references (p.   ) and index.
        ISBN 978-1-61636-325-3 (alk. paper)
1. Lord's Supper—Adoration. 2. Franciscans. I. Franciscan Sisters of Perpetual Adoration
(La Crosse, Wis.)
        BX2233.E834 2012
        264'.02036—dc23
                    2011048752

ISBN 978-1-61636-325-3

Published by St. Anthony Messenger Press
28 W. Liberty St.
Cincinnati, OH 45202
www.AmericanCatholic.org
www.SAMPBooks.org

Printed in the United States of America.
Printed on acid-free paper.

12 13 14 15 16 5 4 3 2 1

CONTENTS

. . . . .

The committee that directed the
creation of this book included:
Jolynn Brehm, FSPA,
Linda Mershon, FSPA,
Julia Walsh, FSPA,
and
Joan Weisenbeck, FSPA.

"In the Sacramental Presence"

In the daily Eucharist we become the body of Christ.
We leave the daily Eucharist to be in communion with all human persons,
with all God's creation, to link with each other, to be the body of Christ.
Perpetual adoration is a continuation of the communion of the Eucharist.
No one of us prays alone; there are always at least two of us.
Always, we honor God in the Sacramental Presence
not only for ourselves, but for our community,
for all those for whom and with whom we minister,
for those who minister to us, for the world community.
In the presence of the Eucharistic Christ, we are fed over and over again;
we are sent over and over again.

In perpetual adoration, we honor, we beg, we thank, we receive,
we minister, we fail, we forgive, we are forgiven,
we are joined in the Loving Presence of God.
Perpetual adoration is a challenge to us to live as we pray:
to live in complete acceptance as Jesus does in the Sacramental Presence;
to work gently, yet strongly against the violence of worldly power;
to live in simplicity in order to feed the world;
to glory in the splendor of our chapel,
but go out to relieve the degradation of the poor;
to live in trust and surrender;
to work to attain justice by recognizing injustice;
to love others as God loves.

—by Helen Koopmann, FSPA

INTRODUCTION

Marlene Weisenbeck, FSPA, and Joan Weisenbeck, FSPA

The Franciscan Sisters of Perpetual Adoration promised their fidelity to Christ in the Blessed Sacrament through a ritual lighting of fire in a humble dish containing lard and a tissue wick. It was all they had when Mother Antonia promised to establish perpetual adoration in 1865. Even today, our hearts are burning within us as we continue to fulfill that promise.

The fire of God's love in our Franciscan tradition is most evidenced in St. Francis' constant adoration. In every church he visited Francis prayed: "We adore You, Lord Jesus Christ, in all Your churches throughout the world, and we bless You, because by Your holy cross You have redeemed the world!"[1] St. Clare followed this intense desire for oneness with the sacrament of the Eucharist. As witnesses of Christ's abiding presence, the Poor Ladies nurtured the feeble faith of commoners, nobles, and outcasts alike. Clare urged her companions to discover the fullness of love by basking in divine light and to become living icons of God.

St. Clare of Assisi does not give us a set of prayers that she created, but in her writings we discover her spirituality and her path to God. She invites us to gaze, consider, contemplate, and imitate Christ. Clare gazes on all of creation because it has the potential to speak to her of God.

She considers the experiences of her life in the light of the Gospels. She contemplates the crucified and glorified Christ and opens herself to be transformed by the Divine One who loves her. She deeply desires to imitate the One she loves to become the image of the Word of Love.

Images of Clare portray her holding the monstrance of the Eucharist, lifting Christ up for all to see. She shows the Most High God to the world. Her vision of Christ is the "brilliance of eternal light / and the mirror without blemish."[2] The purpose of her contemplative prayer is to draw as close as she can to God incarnate so that ultimately she can discover her own unity with God. Then, in her words, we can "taste the hidden sweetness that, from the beginning, God Himself has reserved for His lovers."[3]

Adore the Lord Ceaselessly

Following Christ in the footsteps of Francis and Clare of Assisi, in 1849 fourteen secular Franciscans from Bavaria, Germany, arrived in Milwaukee, Wisconsin, with the intention to found a religious order and serve the immigrants. This religious order became known as the Franciscan Sisters of Perpetual Adoration and was the first religious congregation to establish perpetual adoration in the United States.

In 1865, Mother Antonia in a solemn vow made a promise that, if God would bless the community of sisters, the community would establish perpetual adoration and build a chapel as beautiful as their means would allow. On August 1, 1878, perpetual adoration of the Blessed Sacrament was established in La Crosse, Wisconsin, and has continued uninterrupted to this day. The pledge emanated from the faith of the community's founders in Bavaria, where perpetual adoration had begun in 1674.

This book of reflections witnesses how we, Franciscan Sisters of Perpetual Adoration (FSPA) La Crosse, Wisconsin, come before the Eucharist each hour, every day and night, to gaze, consider, contemplate, and imitate Christ. We seek to become like the One we contemplate and to continually make room for the mystery of God within our lives. We invite you to do the same.

1. Francis of Assisi, "The Testament," in *The Saint,* vol. 1 of *Francis of Assisi: Early Documents,* Regis J. Armstrong, O.F.M. CAP., J.A. Wayne Hellmann, O.F.M. CONV., and William Short, O.F.M., eds. (New York: New City, 1999), pp. 124–125.

2. Clare of Assisi, "The Fourth Letter to Agnes of Prague," *in Clare of Assisi: Early Documents*, Regis J. Armstrong, O.F.M. CAP., ed. and trans. (St. Bonaventure, N.Y.: Franciscan Institute, 1993), p. 50. Hereafter referred to as *CA:ED.*

3. Clare of Assisi, "The Third Letter to Agnes of Prague," *CA:ED*, p. 45.

1 | ESSENTIAL SUSTENANCE

Jean Amlaw, FSPA affiliate

Gaze

"By day they go into towns and villages in order to win others by setting them an example. At night they retire to some hermitage or lonely place and give themselves to meditation."[4]

Consider

We in the twenty-first century think we are the first to be so busy—busy with making money or being students or caring for children, parents, or grandchildren. When we are so busy taking care of people and issues right in front of us, how do we remember to make time to enrich our personal relationship with God? St. Francis, in his own busy life of working, teaching, and writing, was always aware of his need for regular prayer—he would not forget. For Francis, prayer was essential sustenance. His guide was Jesus himself, who invites us through his actions and words to engage in deep dialogue with God. How inviting it is to remember that God calls each of us by name and that our name is written

---

4. Francis of Assisi, *St. Francis of Assisi: Writings and Early Biographies: English Omnibus of the Sources for the Life of St. Francis,* Marion A. Habig, ed. (Cincinnati: St. Anthony Messenger Press, 2008), p. 1829. Hereafter referred to as *Omnibus.*

on the palm of his hand. God wants to be close to us and so sent his Son to be with us, because He loves us. Our part is to remember to make time for God.

Contemplation

Dearest Lord, you know I want to have a deep relationship with you, but I struggle with juggling all of my responsibilities. I forget to pray during my busy day and later I am out of energy. Help me to remember how much you love me and want me to know and love you as well. You have said, "I have called you by name, you are mine," and I realize that you will not forget me. You are always there for me, you pursue me, you whisper in my ear. Help me to discover, as Francis did, the abundant joy and richness you can bring to my life. Amen.

Imitate

Will you make the effort to remember? To remember that building a relationship with God takes time and a commitment to regular communication with him—to talk and to remain silent? Put God into your daily schedule, mark a regular time for your friend. Find a quiet space to be present with God. Allow yourself to be overwhelmed by God's sustaining love.

2 | MY HOPE IS IN CHRIST

Patricia Tekippe, FSPA

Gaze

"By day the LORD commands his steadfast love,
  and at night his song is with me,
  a prayer to the God of my life."

—Psalm 42:8

Consider

One day at the children's Mass in the parish church, a boy named Stevie disagreed with something his mother, Margaret, told him. Although Stevie was a husky twenty-year-old, his mind was four years old. He gave his mother a little shove and quickly she was sprawled in the church aisle. Margaret picked herself up and calmed Stevie while the Mass went on as usual. A few minutes later, as I distributed Communion, Stevie came forward in line and stood before me with tears in his eyes. "I'm sorry, Jesus," he said. What could I do but step forward, give him a hug, and say, "It's OK, Stevie," and offer him the wafer, "Body of Christ"? Pope St. Pius X, a Third Order Franciscan, wrote, "My hope is in Christ, who strengthens the weakest by His divine help."[5] Pius X, called the pope of the Eucharist, changed Church

---

5. Pius X, quoted in Francis Alice Forbes, *Life of Pius X* (London: Burns, Oates and Washbourne, 1918).

regulations to allow the reception of First Holy Communion at an earlier age. He also encouraged frequent reception of the Holy Eucharist at a time when the Jansenist heresy (which discouraged people from receiving) lingered.

Contemplate

Love God, and lead good Christian lives—this was the advice from St. Pius X. Jesus, as I pause today in your presence, enlarge my understanding of what that means. Help me to have the directness of Stevie, who, knowing he had hurt someone who loved him, immediately reached out for forgiveness. Strengthen me in supporting those in our society who are vulnerable; help me live patiently with my own weaknesses. As I walk in your way, I extend my hands to others so that together we can form a safety net. Amen.

Imitate

When your prayer time here is over and you go on your way, how do you experience your own strengths and weaknesses? What opportunities are there to work with others to improve society's attitudes toward people who can't speak up for themselves? Look for ways to stretch across religious differences to make this a safer world for all. Thank God for the goodness in human nature that wants to lift up children and others who can't take care of themselves.

3 | SURRENDER TO MY HEART'S DESIRE

Jeff Dols, FSPA affiliate

Gaze

"Indeed, blessed poverty, holy humility, and inexpressible charity are reflected in that mirror, as, with the grace of God, you can contemplate them throughout the entire mirror."[6]

Consider

What keeps us from seeking our soul's deepest desire? Most often it is the ego and its fear of annihilation. Few of us have the courage to pray as St. Francis did—"Who are you, O God? And who am I?"—because we don't really want to know the answer. While our souls long for intimate unions with God, unions in which we can no longer distinguish our deepest selves from the Divine, our ego selves understand the price of these unions: the loss of our hard-fought external identities. We've spent our entire lives crafting an identity to present to the world, and our egos are terrified at the prospect of that identity being consumed in the flame of God's great love. For if we follow our soul's desire, we will be left standing defenseless and out of control, which is precisely where we need to be to experience the sheer delight and the richness of God's consuming love for us. The Good News for our souls is that the fire of God's love is relentless

---

6. Clare of Assisi, "The Fourth Letter to Agnes of Prague," *CA:ED,* p. 50.

and will eventually break through our well-formed heat shields. When that happens, we too will become a fire of consuming love that draws in everyone around us.

Contemplate

Loving and irresistible God, you draw me into your flame of love, and yet I resist. I pray for the courage to surrender my whole self to you, as St. Francis did, so that, like Francis, I might experience the joy of a life without control, a life that brings the unexpected delights of sweet surrender. Loving God, help me to stop counting the costs and to overcome my fear of loss, so that through your consuming love I may find my true self, transformed by love, ready to share that experience of pure joy through loving service to the world around me. Amen.

Imitate

Look for the many invitations God provides each day to surrender to the flame of love and to serve the reign of God: a simple request to play catch with your son, to go skating with your daughter, to sit with an old friend who is feeling down, to be truly present to the homeless person you encounter on the street, to risk reputation and status and challenge unjust laws and institutions for the sake of the powerless. Each of these opportunities invites you to let go of control, to risk giving yourself away, to let yourself be drawn into the fire of love.

4 | BE THE JESUS PRESENCE

Malinda Gerke, FSPA

Gaze

"We, too, with our own eyes, see only bread and wine, but we must see further and firmly believe that this is his most holy Body and Blood, living and true."[7]

Consider

One of the primary Franciscan traditions is to acknowledge the presence of Jesus in our lives. Both Francis and Clare built their lives around this idea. According to the first admonition of St. Francis, the gift Jesus gave us in the Eucharist is the opportunity to expand the work of the kingdom of God to everyone.

When we participate in the practice of perpetual adoration, we put ourselves in direct contact with the God of presence and mission. Our action as adorers pales in the face of God's action of infusing us with the spirit of the Divine Being. We are changed dramatically just by being in this living presence and being open to the action of our gracious God. We become instruments of God's peace, mercy, joy, consolation, or courage. The more we celebrate the small miracles of daily life, the more we realize the very personal action of God in our daily living.

---

7. Francis of Assisi, "The Admonitions," *Omnibus*, p. 79.

The presence of Jesus among us is just that—a widespread presence among all of God's people. We are able to embed the wonders of the presence of God within us. Each of us can and must be the "Jesus Presence" in this world of ours.

Contemplate

Most loving and considerate Jesus, I thank you for the trust you put in me as you give me the mission to help spread your fragrance everywhere. Help me to recognize your action in my life and to follow your promptings as life unfolds around me. I know that your power will be with me, and that your love will shine through me if I allow you to act. I thank you for all the gifts you have given me. I thank you for delighting that you made me, and I thank you for all those you will send to me this day. Amen.

Imitate

Recognize God's action in your everyday life experiences. In your evening examination of the day, include a listing of the unusual actions of God. Rejoice in the surprises God sends your way.

5 | **TURN FROM ANXIETY TO ADORATION**

Jolynn Brehm, FSPA

Gaze

"I entreat all...to put away every attachment [obstacle], all care and solicitude, and serve, love, honour, and adore our Lord and God with a pure heart and mind."[8]

Consider

Now, in this time, in this space, in this Presence, is the invitation to an essential turning toward God. First, we reflect on the obstacles to overcome. Perhaps the obstacles we face are clutter or schedules, maybe they are prejudices, grudges, or judgments. When we limit any of these things, we turn our focus toward serving, loving, honoring, and adoring the Lord God. Next, the cares and anxieties that often overwhelm us, such as financial, medical, or familial concerns or conflicts, can be put aside in this prayerful, all-loving Presence. As we turn these worries over to God's care, we strive to allow our adoration to strengthen our faith, trust, hope, and compassion.

---

8. Francis of Assisi, "The Rule of 1221," *Omnibus,* p. 48.

Contemplate

Gracious, loving God, help me to be more aware of the obstacles, cares, and anxieties that limit my turning toward you. May I walk the daily path with you, placing my focus on the ways to serve, love, honor, and adore you! Amen.

Imitate

Choose one obstacle to overcome and create a way to turn cares and anxieties into opportunities to entrust all of your life to God.

6 | PERSEVERE IN MY CALLING

Marcia Baumert, FSPA

Gaze

"And loving one another with the charity of Christ, may the love you have in your hearts be shown outwardly in your deeds so that, compelled by such an example, the sisters may always grow in love of God and in charity for one another."[9]

Consider

We each come with our story and unique history; we carry in our bodies the genes of generations present and past. Experiences and relationships bind us to yet a larger story. It is our privilege and responsibility to make choices that nurture and bear witness to our love of God demonstrated by mutual charity.

Clare encouraged her sisters to recognize the dignity of their calling and the possible far-reaching effects of their actions. Rooted in faith and guided by the lives of Jesus and Francis, they learned about and leaned into a lifestyle of simplicity, humility, and poverty. Clare's ageless wisdom encourages us to respect each other as unique as well as interdependent members of the human family. We, too, are reminded that our actions bear potential influence on others.

---

9. Clare of Assisi, "The Testament of Clare," *CA:ED,* p. 60.

Contemplate

Lord, I am called to persevere in my calling. I ponder the ways in which you modeled a life of integrity, compassion, and self-giving love. Help me to remember that we are blessed by the same source of loving energy and creative potential. I desire to embrace dignity and open myself to humbly consider the influence and witness my life might offer to others. I pray that I will allow your grace to empower me and your wisdom to direct my actions. May I be fed in this time of prayer and, by living with joy and gratitude, share what I'm given. Amen.

Imitate

Consider the reputation of your ancestors and current family members and friends. Does your foundation support integrity and goodness? Are there qualities you wish to change as well as those you wish to retain and nurture? Reflect on a time when you were aware of making a difference in the life of another. Focus on a quality of Jesus that you desire and mindfully imitate him. Pay attention to what you notice and allow grace to lead you to share with integrity and mutual charity.

7 | MY GREATEST JOY

Chandra Sherin, FSPA affiliate

Gaze

"Commend me and my sisters to the Lord in your fervent prayers, for we rejoice in the good things of the Lord that He works in you through His grace."[10]

Consider

We can find deep joy in actions of compassion that stretch us beyond our comfort, beliefs, societal norms, and social standing. Francis and Clare found bliss in serving our Lord of compassion with healing, loving action. The struggles and sacrifices they embraced bore abundant fruit in their lives, hearts, and community. Just as Francis found himself loving to serve the lepers who had once seemed a horror, so we have callings to serve in compassion in places and ways that upend our perceptions and perceived social graces in profound ways. Willingness to break past those boundaries of perceived safety and security (with common sense) for the sake of compassionate action, for the love of God and Christ, opens up a new world of profound and abundant joy and graces.

---

10. Clare of Assisi, "The Second Letter to Agnes of Prague," *CA:ED,* p. 43.

Contemplate

Jesus, Holy One, True God of Love and Compassion, Healer and Savior, I enter this silence in reverence for and adoration of your presence, your love, your example. Thank you for your Holy Presence in our lives. We struggle and wrestle daily in our human desire to follow your call. When we reach out to others with compassion, we glimpse the bliss, the abundant joy, and the peace that flows through us and dwells within us. Help us to stretch beyond comfort zones in order to serve you and your creation with compassionate action. May we find within us a love that transforms us beyond our fears and desires to a place of communal joy and reverence for all of life. With courage and trust in you, Lord, we rejoice in your compassion and teachings, as you enrich us beyond measure. Amen.

Imitate

What gives you courage to act compassionately? How can you reach out and serve beyond your comfort zones and sense of security? Recall a time when you experienced tremendous joy in serving others with compassionate action. Sing a song of joy to express this precious feeling. Share joy and fervent prayer in community, linking your heart and mind with Francis and Clare and in praise and adoration of Jesus and our God of compassionate love.

8 | UNITE WITH JESUS' PRESENCE

Marla Lang, FSPA

Gaze

"She [Sister Francesca] also said once, when the sisters believed the blessed mother was at the moment of death and the priest had given her the holy Communion of the body of our Lord Jesus Christ, she, the witness, saw a very great splendor about the head of mother, Saint Clare. It seemed to her the Lord's body was a very small and beautiful young boy. After the holy Mother had received with great devotion and tears, as was her custom, she said these words: 'God has given me such a gift today, that heaven and earth could not equal it.'"[11]

Consider

Simply, presence is a connectedness that happens when we are open to all that is. This open stance can nourish life, make each person more. For example, when we watch the Olympics, we experience the presence of gifted athletes from all over the world in one place. The Olympians amaze us with their skills but even more so the presence that radiates from them in the forms of encouragement, connection, interaction, and celebration of one another amaze us. The

---

11. "The Acts of the Process of Canonization of Clare of Assisi," *CA:ED,* p. 167.

athletes transform us. Their energy flows even through cameras and into televisions in our homes.

Contemplate

O God of relationships, you taught me about expressed presence—that where two or three are gathered in God's name, you are there in the midst. Help me to be open, to know you are with me. I want to be united with your presence, as you long to hear my yearnings. Fill my spirit with your love. Amen.

Imitate

Today as you move about daily tasks and engagements, be open to the gift of presence as found in Clare of Assisi, Olympic athletes, the Eucharistic Christ, and all those you meet. May this presence be the daily bread you most need.

9 | BETWEEN MY SOUL AND GOD

Marla Lang, FSPA

Gaze

"Look at God…my brothers, and *pour out your hearts before him*."[12]

Consider

On May 21, 2011, Pope Benedict XVI questioned astronauts huddled before a camera in the international space shuttle while in orbit around the earth. He wanted to be further enlightened by their unique vantage point. Flying over continents and oceans, the astronauts contemplated the earth without any boundaries of separation cradled in the universe.

As we consider these cosmic perspectives before the vantage point of Eucharistic presence, we must also consider our own awareness that overwhelms us. Notice how God is hidden and yet the source of all radiant energy in the earth's mysteries. Yes, God is humbly present in the simple piece of bread, in the far-off galaxy, in your neighbor's heart.

12. Francis of Assisi, "Letter to a General Chapter," *Omnibus*, p. 106.

Contemplate

Jesus, I come before you today in silence, attentive to the many expressions of your hidden presence in all creation. You even humbled your very essence to become human, a creature like ourselves, so I might better know you. I know I am incapable of fully comprehending your self-emptying presence found everywhere I turn. The mystics before me rested their awe and questions in you. So, I come before you today with a desiring heart. And, like Pope Benedict, I seek further insights. Amen.

Imitate

As you make your way to work, to classrooms, to national parks, to the night sky, pay attention to your "adoration" vantage point. How has God chosen to be hidden in all that is? How do your actions show that you believe that? Thank God for being so humble and so comfortable in your soul every day.

10 | THE MIRROR OF ETERNITY

Jean Kasparbauer, FSPA

Gaze

"Place your mind before the mirror of eternity!
Place your soul in the brilliance of glory!
Place your heart in the figure of the divine substance."[13]

Consider

St. Clare of Assisi wrote to Agnes: "Place your mind before the mirror of eternity!" We may wonder how we can do that. We may wonder how to calm our minds enough to see the reflection of Divine Love.

One way is to breathe slowly and breathe again slowly, and breathe again deeply. Focusing without too much effort, just breathe again, again, and again. Believe that the Loving Presence thrives on stillness. Stillness blossoms into adoration. Adoration longs for Loving Presence. With longing, place our minds before the mirror of eternity.

The world today can be blessed by those who breathe a peaceful vibration into the atmosphere. A "distraction" could be calling us to take what is coming to mind and bless it so that we can place it before the mirror of eternity. We must breathe now—breathe again and again. We must be still…and place our minds before the mirror of eternity.

---

13. Clare of Assisi, "The Third Letter to Agnes of Prague," *CA:ED,* p. 45.

Contemplate

O Loving Presence,
please still my heart so my eyes can see.
Still my mind so that wisdom can come.
Still my body so that Divine Love can grow.
Still my desires so that Christ is manifested in the universe.

O Loving Presence,
please still my heart so my eyes can see.
Still my mind so that wisdom can come to me.
Still my body so that Divine Love can grow.
Still my desires so that the universe becomes a mirror of
   eternity.

Imitate

When you leave adoration, take time to breathe—at the red light, in the long grocery line, and so on. When your mind seems cluttered, remember to breathe and bring stillness into your life and into the universe. When you find yourself racing around, breathe and slow your body so adoration can blossom.

11 | CONNECT WITH THE WORLD, EXULT WITH THE HEAVENS

by Jean Kasparbauer, FSPA

Gaze

"Our whole being should be seized with fear, the whole world should tremble and heaven rejoice, when Christ the Son of the Living God is present."[14]

Consider

We spend time in prayer to do what St. Francis of Assisi asked his followers to do just before he died. With Francis, we desire to connect with the world through our prayer and to exult with the heavens by our lives. We praise Christ present on the altar of our churches and in everyone we meet. We adore the body of Christ present in the hungry of the world. We share the blood of Christ when we assist the poor and suffering in the world.

With delight, we exult with the amazing creatures in the depths of the sea. With awe and wonder, we praise the living God, Loving Presence, in the expanding universe. In all the atoms, molecules, waves, and particles of light, we give glory to the living God by our lives and by our prayer.

---

14. Francis of Assisi, "Letter to a General Chapter," *Omnibus,* p. 105.

Contemplate

O Loving Presence, we adore you on the altars of worship.
O Loving Presence, we praise you on the altar of the earth.
O Loving Presence, we stand in awe at the wonders and
mystery of the universe.

May we know the wonder of your love in the Eucharist.
May we treasure all peoples of the earth.
May we tremble with delight at the galaxies of the heavens.

We adore you, O Loving Presence, every day of our lives.

Imitate

Today, tomorrow, and the next day, be intent when you awake to adore Christ with a loving thought, to exult with a gracious greeting the living God in your neighbor, and to offer praise when you stand in awe of a sunset or a thundercloud. What do you plan to do in order to live each day in wonder and awe of Loving Presence?

12 | EMBRACE TRANSFORMATION

Rose Elsbernd, FSPA

Gaze

"And transform your entire being into the image of the Godhead Itself through contemplation."[15]

Consider

Transforming seems like an action that we must do. Rather, in the quiet, we let go. We do not work. Through the quiet of adoration we come to know even deeper the relational aspects of who we are as the created in the image of God. We are the image of God. We are one with the One. We awaken to the refreshing, peaceful, and healing elements of God within our very being. It is contemplation that envelopes us in the "largeness" of the now. Awareness draws us into "the More." Becoming "More" moves us outward to embrace the transforming aspects of touching those who are hurting, working to correct the systems of oppression, and advocating for the "little ones." The call to respond is clear: Go and be God's hands, God's voice, and God's love for all.

---

15. Clare of Assisi, "The Third Letter to Agnes of Prague," *CA:ED,* p. 45.

Contemplate

Loving One, you call me time and time again to accept my true identity. Sometimes, I would rather shun the full implications of my being and live in a manner that makes me "small" and therefore inadequate to respond to the needs of this day. Forgive me and keep pestering me with the true message! I do yearn to accept the quiet transformation of my "entire being into the image of the Godhead Itself." May it be done. Amen.

Imitate

Pay attention to the times throughout the day when you make a comment that indicates that you are not enough. Dismiss each negative thought with a positive acclamation of your goodness. Look at your fear in terms of taking a stand regarding social issues. What are the roots of your fear and how do they relate to the above meditation?

13 | PRAY ALWAYS

Sarah Hennessey, FSPA

Gaze

"Let us adore him with a pure heart."[16]

Consider

"What if the whole chapel was going to disappear in ten seconds and we could each take only one thing?" Out of curiosity, I went around the convent asking this question. Most sisters said, "The monstrance." One sister said she would take that beautiful stained-glass window of the seraphim. Then someone said, "I would keep the sister praying beside me." In our Franciscan chapel we always pray in pairs. My sister is the one who reveals Christ to me and helps me to not lose heart. Trust is deepened not only with the gaze upon the Blessed Sacrament but through the very real flesh of interaction. Our adoration becomes the practice of forgiveness and celebration as we forgive our human failings and celebrate the God within one another.

16. Francis of Assisi, "The Rule of 1221," *Omnibus*, p. 49.

Contemplate

Loving God of my heart, I am never alone in you. I am never abandoned. May my trust be tried by the fire of your love and grow through the daily interactions with my brothers and sisters. You promise not to take away my fears and doubts but always to renew my heart and mind. May I live each day as prayer and not give up hope. Amen.

Imitate

List the ways that you pray always in your daily life. Who has been your prayer today? What do you need to forgive or ask forgiveness for? How are you thankful? Who becomes Eucharist for you?

14 | BODIES, NOW GATHER

Julia Walsh, FSPA

Gaze

"And so it is really the spirit of God who dwells in his faithful who receive the most holy Body and Blood of our Lord."[17]

Consider

All over earth we gather as church. Our bodies are in different chapels to adore our precious God. We have traveled like pilgrims to have a moment to be quiet with our God. St. Francis also prayed with his body—and ultimately was blessed with the stigmata. The pain from the stigmata deepened his belief in the goodness of God. Our bodies hurt. Our feet are heavy. We ache from the stress and tension of living in a complex world. We have scars, wounds, bruises, scratches. We are broken. Our souls spiral with fears and concerns. Questions can crush us, but yet we are gathered here to just be. Let's just be. While we are, we remember we are Christ's body. We're together, we're united. We pray with our bodies as we adore God. We bow, kneel, and stand. We squirm in our seats and smile in our rejoicing. Our breathing deepens as we meditate and begin to sense the presence of Jesus. As we quiet, we gain great awe: somehow, we are all God's body.

---

17. Francis of Assisi, "The Admonitions," *Omnibus,* p. 78.

Contemplate

Jesus, you know that I have come through a lot to get here to be with you today. I am glad to pray and be with you, but my body feels so broken and tired. I gain comfort, Jesus, in knowing that you also had a very human body, and it is good. I know I am not alone with you, God, and that is my joy. Throughout this world many faithful people are also in prayer at this exact moment. We are united and gathered together in the wide mystery of your love. I trust that we really are your body in this world today. I pray that you help us act like it. Amen.

Imitate

After you end your prayer here, pay attention to the sacredness of human bodies. Do you see people hurting? Do you appreciate the beauty of bodies? Can you help, heal, listen, love, or serve another human body? As you move your body, notice how you are united with others. Thank God for how all bodies are working together for the kingdom of God.

15 | ADMIRE GOD'S CREATIVE AND GENEROUS ABILITIES

Pauline Wittry, FSPA

Gaze

"Praise him and bless him, thank and adore him, the Lord almighty, in Trinity and Unity."[18]

Consider

As we look around us in the cathedral of nature, we see so much beauty—the green trees, the blooming flowers of late summer, and the flowing water of our rivers and lakes. Where did they originate? Who designed them? How did they come to be here? Have we ever looked at a blade of grass in all its simplicity? Why has one flower five petals and another ten or even twenty or more? Why do roses have thorns and pansies do not? Trees come in so many different forms. Some have needles and others have leaves. Even the bark differs from one tree to another. Red pine trees have red on their bark while white pine trees have white on their cones. Think of all the varieties of maple, oak, elm, and birch trees. The difference between trees and shrubs, the varying age of trees in the woods—all mirror the creative and generous abilities of our God.

---

18. Francis of Assisi, "The Rule of 1221," *Omnibus*, p. 47.

Contemplate

Jesus, thanks and praise rise naturally on my lips as I look at all that surrounds me while I sit in adoration. Your generosity, O God, is so great—surpassing anything I could possibly imagine. How did you put all this together in these few acres? Francis expressed his praise in his "Canticle of the Creatures." Somehow, I can only say thanks and thanks again. Trying to express this beauty in a painting or in words seems so futile. I do not know how to paint the light coming off the water in sparkling diamonds or the subtle differences in the trees. How can I describe them so others can see? Photos can pick up some of the beauty but not all. It needs to be experienced. Thank you. Amen.

Imitate

How can you appreciate nature more and help others to celebrate the beauty of grass and the trees? Could you invite others to just sit and look around them at the nature that is present? Even in the city? Could you place a pot of flowers or a bouquet from the grocery store in your window so others might see and have their spirits lifted a bit? Write your own canticle of praise like Francis' to give God praise and thanks, perhaps something like: "Praise you, O God, for our little lake, its trees, its reeds and ducks, geese and loons. We thank you and give you praise for all that you have made, O God, Trinity and Unity."

16 | JESUS ALL AROUND ME

Leclare Beres, FSPA

Gaze

"Happy, indeed, is she…
  Whose affection excites,
  Whose contemplation refreshes,
  Whose kindness fulfills,
  Whose delight replenishes."[19]

Consider

We live in a world filled with busy people who hustle and bustle about, some firmly planted, others finding their way. Let us take a few moments to quiet ourselves and look for God amid all this. For a brief period reflect on God's beautiful creation, the deep blue sky, the tall trees with branches waving in the wind, the many flowers with a richness of colors showing their beauty. Listen for the water quietly running over the rocks; listen to the birds singing and the animals moving about, munching the grass. Be still and look about; all of God's beauty is there for us. Now reflect on the words of Clare as we put ourselves in Christ's presence. We know that Jesus gave his entire life because of great love for each of us and the whole world. Let us continue to quiet

---

19. Clare of Assisi, "The Fourth Letter to Agnes of Prague," *CA:ED,* p. 50.

ourselves and reflect on Jesus within and all around us. Listen as he speaks to us.

Contemplate

Jesus, it is my wish to spend time with you, to open my heart and soul to praise you, to thank you for what you have done for me. I ask you to guide me in all I do, to be ever mindful of your goodness and your gift of self. I need you and ask you to bless me, my family and friends, and the whole world.

Imitate

As you leave the Divine Presence, be mindful of and listen to people hurting and in need of divine care. Reach out and touch them so that they may experience God's love and care. Let them know of God's everlasting love.

17 | PREACH BY EXAMPLE

Jolynn Brehm, FSPA

Gaze

"All the friars, however, should preach by their example."[20]

Consider

Words, words, words! Imagine the amount of words that fill every day! Perhaps the multitude of words are overwhelming, annoying, just filling space. Perhaps the value, meaning, and importance of words deserve attention. In this Divine Eucharistic Presence, no words are needed. Lingering in solitude, quiet, and the "now" moment provides peace, calm, and deeper awareness of Divine Love for all our world. St. Francis seemed to have a profound intuition about the powerful impact of wordless presence. All are invited to go among the people and into all of creation with a sacred presence, a preaching through the reverence and awe of deeds. A gift of Eucharistic Adoration may be to cultivate a respect for words and an even fuller appreciation of the influence of mindful, wordless deeds as each day is lived with our union with Christ.

---

20. Francis of Assisi, "The Rule of 1221," *Omnibus,* p. 44.

Contemplate

O Eucharistic Christ, your wordless presence to me is a profound and moving reminder that I am to "preach the Good News" by the deeds of my life. Grant me a deeper respect for words if and when they are needed or necessary. Amen.

Imitate

When have you experienced meaningful silence? When do you think many words are more efficient? Decide each day when and how words are truly meaningful, thoughtful, and life-giving.

18 | GIVE TOTALLY TO GOD

Antona Schedlo, FSPA

Gaze

"[She was] continually occupying her soul
with sacred prayers and divine praises.
She had already focused
the most fervent attention of her entire desire on the Light
and she opened more generously the depths of her mind
to the torrents of grace
that bathe a world of turbulent change."[21]

Consider

As Clare of Assisi opened herself more generously to grace, so did another young woman also named Clare: Clare of Rimini, Italy. Bl. Clare of Rimini lost her mother when she was seven. Her father could not devote much time to her. Consequently, she grew up a frivolous young woman. The man she married was also lost in worldly pleasures. One day while attending Mass in her usual, distracted way, Clare felt the urge to say at least one prayer with great devotion. Reciting the Our Father, she felt her soul become enlightened, and she saw the frightful state of her life. Trembling in fear, she firmly resolved to change. She entered

---

21. "The Legend of St. Clare," *CA:ED,* pp. 273–274.

the Secular Franciscans. After her husband died, she lived a strict life of prayer, penance, and charity. Remembering her past, Clare encouraged young women to avoid vanity and worldliness. Consider how both Clares avoided the lure of worldly pleasures to give themselves totally to God and others.

Contemplate

Lord, as I contemplate you, the source of all goodness, in the Blessed Sacrament, and the Eucharist, fill my life with your brilliant light that I may turn from worldly, frivolous pleasures and serve you faithfully. Only then can true joy be found. I ask this through Jesus, the knowing Christ. Amen.

Imitate

Today when you feel lured to worldly, sinful pleasures, try to recall Bl. Clare of Rimini and devoutly say a prayer asking God to lead you to a healthier, more wholesome life.

19 | **FURNACE OF LOVE**

Joan Weisenbeck, FSPA

Gaze

"When Brother Juniper appeared among them, that excellent jester of the Lord who uttered the Lord's words which were often warming, she was filled with a new joy and asked him if he had had anything new from the Lord. When he opened his mouth, he burst forth with words that were like burning sparks coming from the furnace of his fervent heart. The virgin of the Lord took great comfort in his parables."[22]

Consider

When we contemplate the Eucharist, we contemplate the heart of Christ that has loved us to the extreme. Christ transforms the hardness of human hearts by offering to each of us the power of his love. Because Brother Juniper was on fire with God's love, the words that came from him to others were like sparks that inspired and moved others. Jesus spoke these words to St. Margaret Mary: "My divine heart is so inflamed with love for all people that being unable any longer to contain within itself the flames of its burning charity, it must spread them abroad and manifest itself to them in order to enrich them with the precious treasures of

---

22. "The Legend of St. Clare," *CA:ED,* p. 295.

my Heart."[23] We are invited each day to enter into the fire of love of the heart of the Eucharistic Jesus and to consider what kind of a heart transplant we need to be the instruments of God's love in the world.

Contemplate

Furnace of Divine Love, Gift of your Eucharistic Heart,
fiery is your glow, illuminating is your light, purifying is
  your love.
Warm the coldness of my heart. Burn your love deep within
  my soul.
Set me on fire for gospel living. Enfold my heart within
  yours!

Imitate

Make a conscious effort throughout the day to reflect the fire of God's love in your heart through goodness, joy, forgiveness, peace, and prayer.

---

23. Margaret Mary Alacoque, letter to John Croiset, s.j. (November 2, 1689), in *The Letters of St. Margaret Mary Alaocque,* Clarence A. Herbst, ed. (Charlotte, N.C.: TAN, 2009).

20 | **DIVINE WHISPERS**

Joan Weisenbeck, FSPA

Gaze

"But after the others went to their hard beds to rest their tired bodies, she remained in prayer, thoroughly vigilant and invincible, so that she could then secretly receive the divine whispers while sleep occupied the others."[24]

Consider

All of us long for a spiritual road map to guide us along life's journey. St. Clare of Assisi was fully aware of her connection to the Divine. She knew that, in the stillness and deep silence of the night, she could listen to the whispers of God's guidance within her heart. Contemplation was Clare's refreshment, always making fresh again her intimacy with the Lord Jesus. This guidance is within all of us, speaking to us in whispers. But it is only when we set aside the dramas, the busyness that life brings, that we can hear and feel these divine whispers of guidance. When we clear our minds of the clutter in life, we have the opportunity to connect with the Divine. A deeper spiritual self is within us. When we find that connection to our deeper self, we find a connection with the Divine. God invites us to be still for a time each day.

24. "The Legend of St. Clare," *CA:ED*, p. 274.

In the mystery of this time spent, God brings us to newness. God lovingly calls each of us, and sometimes even at night, to surrender into the mystery of this stillness.

Contemplate

God, send me help from the holy dwelling place, from the divine abode within me. Give me my heart's deepest desires and fulfill all of my dreams and answer me from the holy dwelling within us. Amen.

Imitate

How are you open to receive the divine whispers in your life? Can you catch the stirrings of the Spirit as you keep the vigil of mystery before the Eucharistic Presence? Put your ears to the wall of your heart and listen there for the whispers of knowing. Love will touch you if you are very still.

21 | WORSHIP IN SPIRIT AND TRUTH

Marlene Weisenbeck, FSPA

Gaze

"It is such…as these the Father claims as his worshippers. *God is spirit, and they who worship him, must worship in spirit and truth* (Jn 4:24)."[25]

Consider

From within our very being, God's Spirit calls us to adoration. We find the very source of adoration within us, for God dwells in us. Scripture confirms that we are made in God's image (see Genesis 1:27). We know this in a primordial way if we but open ourselves to a conscious acknowledgment of God's Spirit present within us. We must go deep inside to a place where God will speak to us in the silence of God's song. Understanding this oneness with divinity then will bring us to assert ourselves in adoration before the all-holy God. In adoring our loving God, we are doing what is most natural to us, and it is therefore essentially an experience of what is most true. In adoration we will become one with God's song. As God's Spirit entered the hearts of Francis and Clare to live a joyful gospel life of love through justice, so we too can expect this Spirit to reveal God's call to justice in our midst.

---

25. Francis of Assisi, "The Rule of 1221," *Omnibus,* p. 49.

Contemplate

Spirit of God, you lure me into solitude, where you awake eager longings deep within my soul. Gentle my heart to welcome you within me, O God. Awaken in me deeper desire for God-life. Breathe in me, O beautiful Spirit, the stirrings of new life and the freedom to surrender to your embrace. Spirit of God, fill me with the fire of your love. Touch my heart, my mind, and my soul so that I might dare to bow to the needs of this world. God of truth, bring to birth in me your mission of overflowing goodness and love. Amen.

Imitate

To whom do you belong? For what purpose? When you answer this truthfully, then your stance before God can be nothing but adoration of the God within and the God without. As you believe more fully in God's goodness and God's indwelling Spirit, then you will view all creation as gifts of the All-Good God who with infinite passion cares for all that is given. Considering God's passion for creation, do you limit your passion for gratitude? Express your gratitude this week by establishing a right relationship with someone in need.

22 | COME TO BELIEVE IN LOVE

Celesta Day, FSPA

Gaze

"We must love God, then, and adore him with a pure heart and mind, because this is what he seeks above all else."[26]

Consider

We declare love in our prayers. We are taught that we are loved by God. But how do we love? Francis followed his heart when he turned toward his burning love of God. Clare admired Francis and fled from her family's wishes to pursue her love of God with her sisters. They purified their lives and followed the desires of their hearts to adore God. Elizabeth of Hungary did the same. After becoming a widow, she left her castle and began to care for the ill and the poor as one of the first secular Franciscans. Her story is captured in the phrase "we have come to believe in love," which serves as title of the letter published by the Franciscans to commemorate the eighth centenary of her birth. How completely they— Clare, Francis, Elizabeth—made their choices. They each honored their responsibilities but found ways to express the deepest commitment of their lives, to love and adore their

---

26. Francis of Assisi, "Letter to All the Faithful," *Omnibus,* p. 94.

God. They must have listened intensely to the desires of their hearts to overcome the other demands of their lives.

Contemplate

God, who is the source of all being, all desires, and all of life, how intimately you call to me. You have pulled souls toward yourself throughout the centuries, and now you speak to me. Thank you for your presence, Spirit of Truth and Father of us all. I ask your help in purifying my heart and my mind, you who know all things. You are the ultimate of goodness and truth. I can only adore in amazement and joy the reality of your care for the greatness of creation and the smallness of me. I praise the Spirit that is so near, so dear. May you be praised by all you have created.

Imitate

Practice remembering that each person you meet is being drawn toward their God and maker. Try to demonstrate your awareness of God's love with your gratitude and appreciation for all of creation. With God's help and support, follow the desires that surface when you see opportunities to serve others. Within God's encompassing presence, return to God your small flame of adoration and love.

23 | GIVE THANKS FOR GOD'S GOODNESS

Betty Shakal, FSPA

Gaze

"You may totally love Him [Christ]
Who gave Himself totally for your love."[27]

Consider

Each day we are surrounded and inundated by the goodness of God's love—we see the blue skies and the beauty of creation, the green trees and the multicolored flowers. We open our eyes and realize the solidity of the bricks and mortar. We view the puffy white clouds floating by and know and recognize the gift of the waters of the rivers and streams. We see and sense the gift of food and drink, the warmth of clothes, and the comfort of a bed. Then we remember that God gives himself to us and continues to do so every day in Holy Mass. We are in awe of the work of our God and speechless when we think of the kindness and the generosity God has shown us each and every day!

---

27. Clare of Assisi, "The Third Letter to Agnes of Prague," *CA:ED,* p. 46.

Contemplate

Thank you, God, for your goodness to me. Thank you, Jesus, for your gifts and your great kindness. You know I am distracted by the work that you have given me to do. You know that I want to love you as you deserve to be loved. You know that I want to serve you with my whole heart and soul. And you know that my attention span is short and that my body's aches and pains remind me that I am terribly weak and powerless. You know that I do want to serve you well. You know that my weak human condition prevents me from giving you my all. And you know that I am unable to love you as I ought, but that I would if only I could. Amen.

Imitate

Give thanks for God's great love and care! Give thanks for the beauty of the world God has given you! Give thanks for God's great goodness! God is so good! All the time!

24 | THE PRIVILEGE OF POVERTY

Betty Shakal, FSPA

Gaze

"O God-centered Poverty,
whom the Lord Jesus Christ
  Who ruled and now rules heaven and earth,
  Who spoke and all things were made,
    condescended to embrace before all else."[28]

Consider

Clare wrote a series of letters to her friend Agnes, princess of Prague, before her entrance into religious life. Clare writes to her about the poverty she had learned from Francis. Poverty was very dear to Clare because she wanted to give her full attention to God. In an age when upper-class women who depended on their dowries had servants who took care of all temporal cares and menial duties, Clare invented a gospel lifestyle marked by sisterly communion, prayer, and manual labor. The sisters depended on their needlework and on the vegetables they grew in their small garden plots. Actual physical poverty—having nothing—fostered their union with God. For Clare, holy poverty was an expression of her total union with God. It became the central work of her life

---

28. Clare of Assisi, "The First Letter to Agnes of Prague," *CA:ED,* p. 36.

to see that the right and privilege to live with nothing of one's own would be assured to her sisters forever.

Contemplate

Jesus, you know how Clare's practice and example of poverty challenges me, even as it challenged Agnes. And you know how her generosity scares me. Yet, the example of Jesus and of Francis and Clare continues to draw me. Jesus came into the world with nothing and lay in a manger meant for the animals. As Matthew writes: "Foxes have holes, and birds of the air have nests; but the Son of Man has nowhere to lay his head" (8:20). Jesus, be the center of my life. Let me follow your example, and be free to love. Amen.

Imitate

Reflect on Clare's poverty and also upon the challenge she places before Agnes to accept poverty. What challenge does she place before you? How will you answer it?

25 | HONOR MY BREATHPRINT

Suzanne Rubenbauer, FSPA

Gaze

"Gaze upon that mirror each day,…and continually study your face within it."[29]

Consider

Clare of Assisi was a realist. Though in a cloister, she knew how the world operated and how easy it was and is for a person to lose track of her heart, her devotion to God. Daily responsibilities and events if not reflected upon have the potential of sidetracking us from the core of who we really are as daughters and sons of the living God. In this letter to Agnes, Clare urges Agnes to remain faithful to her relationship to God. When we gaze on the mirror of reality that daily prayer offers, God is the center, the mirror who reflects back our reality and our own unique inner beauty. Nothing else gets in the way. We can then reflect back the goodness of God.

---

29. Clare of Assisi, "The Fourth Letter to Agnes of Prague," *CA:ED,* p. 50.

Contemplate

Most gracious and kind God, as I sit with you today in prayer, help me to remember that it is you that I seek. Your face, your heart, your wisdom lives within me because I am your daughter, your son. My breath is your breath. I am your living presence. May my devotion to you spill out into the world, reflecting your love and presence. Thank you for being the originator and sustainer of all love. Amen.

Imitate

During your prayer today, gaze on your breath by simply paying attention to it. Just as every person has a thumbprint, so each of us has a breathprint. It started when we took our first God-given breath. After prayer and during the rest of the day, continue to gaze on your breath by being aware of it. In times of anxiety or during a stressful part of your day, go back to your God-given breath. Gaze upon God by honoring your breath.

26 | LIVE THE LIFE OF THE GOSPEL

Jean Moore, FSPA

Gaze

"When God gave me some friars, there was no one to tell me what I should do; but the Most High himself made it clear to me that I must live the life of the Gospel."[30]

Consider

When Francis of Assisi was searching for meaning and direction in his life, he prayed before the crucifix in the little church of San Damiano. He heard God tell him to "rebuild his house." During his life dedicated to living the gospel, Francis came to recognize the Divine Presence in all people and all of creation, and he reverenced all because all that comes from God is gift.

St. Rose of Viterbo was a young woman who listened to the preaching of the Franciscan friars at Mass and attuned her soul to listen to the Divine Presence within her. Because of the strength and faith she received from her prayer and adoration, she spoke against the societal injustices and political conflicts in her town and encouraged people to remain faithful to God in their actions and thoughts. To live the gospel, we, too, must listen to God in prayer and adoration.

---

30. Francis of Assisi, "The Testament of St. Francis," *Omnibus,* p. 68.

Contemplate

Loving God, you asked Francis to "rebuild" your house because it was "falling into ruin." When I listen to the news, I think that our world is falling into ruin, and I feel helpless to fix it. You ask me, however, not to solve all of the world's problems but rather to live my life as Jesus did: to "rebuild your house" through my own prayer and actions. Building a house is a slow process of one brick at a time, one wall at a time, mortared carefully and diligently. Perhaps you are asking me to ponder the gifts you have given me (my bricks) and the ways I can use my gifts (the cement) to rebuild your house of justice and right relationships. Help me, God, to see you in all people, especially within myself, so that I might bring your Divine Presence into this world on a daily basis.

Imitate

Spend time listening to God with an open heart and keen senses. What gifts do you have for bringing God's goodness into your life and the world around you? How has God gifted you with goodness or kindness or hope or love? Where, or in whom, do you experience the presence of God in your life? How is God calling you to bring God's Divine Presence to others around you and in the world?

27 | GOD'S GOODNESS IN ALL CREATION

Paulynn Instenes, FSPA

Gaze

"What wonderful majesty! What stupendous condescension! O sublime humility! O humble sublimity! That the Lord of the whole universe, God and the Son of God, should humble himself like this and hide under the form of a little bread, for our salvation."[31]

Consider

What do we see when we look at the bread of the Eucharist? Do we see a God who loves us so much that he feeds us with the very bread of life? Are we in awe of this God who speaks to us in such simple terms, a God who proclaims himself to be an incarnational God, a God who dwells within each of us? How do we show reverence for such a God? St. Francis saw the goodness of God in all of creation. For St. Francis, adoration became a litany of gratitude. He treated all creation as a reflection of God and in so doing he showed great respect and humility toward all.

---

31. Francis of Assisi, "Letter to a General Chapter," *Omnibus,* pp. 105–106.

Contemplate

God of my heart, God who loves me above all, I humbly thank you for all the gifts you have given me. Your creation, your Son, and the Spirit have all been part of my life and have lifted me up and held me close to you. Thank you for all the gifts you have given me through my family, friends, and others who helped me see you. I humbly beg for your grace to see and respect all, to be more grateful for all that I receive today. You are my God and I am yours. Amen.

Imitate

Today remember to be respectful to all people who cross your path. Remember that you are called to be the bread for others. What can you do to give nourishment to others today? Be the voice of good news today. Remember to thank God for all the gifts you receive. Give praise and glory to God.

28 | FRANCISCAN JOY

Wendie Libert, FSPA affiliate

Gaze

"How holy and beloved, how pleasing and lowly, how peaceful, delightful, lovable and desirable above all things it is to have a Brother [Jesus] like this."[32]

Consider

There is no such thing as a party of one. There is no "alone" within God's mandate to love: no lover without the beloved, no parent without a child, no brother without a sister, no husband without a wife.

Francis of Assisi names our interconnection when he writes that we become brothers when we do God's will, spouses when our souls are wed to Christ through the Spirit, and mothers when we give birth to Christ through holy works. The fullest experience of Eucharist, then, and the holy joy of adoration, flows from the jubilant, dancing, soaring cosmic celebration of the "kingdom" that unfolds before us when we seek divine love in one another.

---

32. Francis of Assisi, "Letter to All the Faithful," *Omnibus,* p. 96.

Contemplate

O holy Dance, waltz as the sacredness in each of our
neighbors;

O loving Song, resolve the dissonant chords of intolerance
and sing your melody in our hearts;

O pleasing Vow, bind firm the pledge to be our sisters' and
brothers' keepers;

O humble Feast, palate of unity, nourish wisdom in the
midst of those who disagree;

O peaceful Celebration, gaze upon this aching creation
with your soft eyes;

O sweet Kiss, sustain the passion of your servants who tend
the lepers of our world;

O lovable Embrace, enfold our enemies in the fullness of
your grace;

O Source, O Son and Brother, O Holy Breath, desirable
above all things, make complete your Sacrament in us.

Imitate

How are you called to celebrate? Whom are you to adore?
Who brings Christ, Real and Present, to you today, and to
whom are you asked to bring Christ's presence? Look into
the eyes of those around you—family, friends, colleagues,
enemies, and strangers—and consciously offer Eucharist
with your smile, your words, your touch, and your
compassionate, active presence.

29 | PRAISE GOD ALL DAY LONG

Elizabeth Brendel, FSPA prayer partner

Gaze

"Happy are those who live in your house,
ever singing your praise."

—Psalm 84:4

Consider

In a novel, a young homemaker and recluse who is struggling with depression and lamenting the mundane sadness of her life untypically receives a visitor into her home. The depressed woman is intrigued by the visitor's unique character and presumptuously friendly spirit. As the story evolves, it's revealed that the stranger is Mary, the mother of Jesus; however, the homemaker does not recognize Mary, because she is dressed in contemporary clothing and engages joyfully in routine duties such as mending and washing clothes. What happened to the young homemaker in the novel? She was transformed by this visitor and formed a joyful relationship with Mary long before she determined who it might be. She blossomed as Mary complimented her, recognized her worth, and listened to her fears, and together they laughed as they carried out routine duties around the house. As in this story, we, too, can become more joyful if we do our work while praising the Lord.

Contemplate

In Psalm 84, praise is for you, Lord, and it joyfully expresses the longing for this happy union of belonging to your "house." May I also welcome you into my "house" and become enriched by your presence within me. Help me to praise you all day long as I view my activities as oneness with you. Amen.

Imitate

Today try to be more "interruptible," and so welcome others to feel the joy of a supporting relationship. Consciously find something joyful in all your tasks today while praising God for each opportunity.

30 | BUILD UP IN LOVE

Dorothy Dunbar, FSPA

Gaze

"Blessed that friar who loves and respects his brother…[and] would not say anything behind his back that he could not say charitably to his face."[33]

Consider

Jesus commanded Francis, "Rebuild my Church." Rebuild, not tear down. At times we say hurtful or judgmental words. We are wounded, we wound. We all need healing, love, and forgiveness. In the presence of Eucharistic Love, we have experienced these gifts. Then we are challenged to bring them to others. Our words are softened, our hearts are moved. We become more like the One we adore. As our prayer deepens, we understand we are all in the same imperfect family. Even when confronting another, we know that our lips and heart, touched in adoration, must respond in kindness. Every time this happens, the Body of Christ is built up in love. Our words can hurt or heal but, strengthened in prayer, we can choose to be builders of God's family.

33. Francis of Assisi, "The Admonitions," *Omnibus*, p. 86.

Contemplate

Eucharistic Christ, you receive me with open arms. I need you. There are words I wished I had said and those I wished I hadn't. Even if I didn't say everything I thought, I admit that I've often been judgmental. I turn to you as a mirror in which I see myself as I really am. You love me exactly as I am while calling me to grow. May I be so touched by you that my words reflect your love and forgiveness. Amen.

Imitate

What do you say when you interact with another? Are you kind or judgmental? Do you see each person as a brother or sister? Remember a time when someone's gentle words helped ease your pain. Remember a time when your words soothed another. Thank God that you are called to build up the Body of Christ in love.

31 | BE PRAISED, BROTHER SUN AND SISTER MOON

Kristin Peters, FSPA

Gaze

Every creature in heaven and on earth and in the depths of the sea should give God praise and glory and honor and blessing.[34]

Consider

The outpouring of God's goodness is love that flows abundantly, that generates and gives forth the life of the Word.

Look to creation and consider the branches of a tree bursting forth from a seed. As the tree matures and reaches deeper into the earth and higher into the sky, its branches twist and reach outward, and the trunk widens to support the branches that enable the tree to thrive. Delicate buds, flowers, and leaves burst forth as an integral and necessary support for the life of the tree. It is a beautifully functioning system.

Sit by a tree, consider the way the tree relates with all creation, with Brother Sun, Sister Moon, Brothers Wind and Air and every kind of weather, Sister Water, and Sister

---

34. Paraphrase of "The Canticle of Brother Sun" by Francis of Assisi, *Omnibus,* pp. 130–131.

Earth, our mother, who nourishes and sustains us. As St. Francis prayed, so can we:

"All praise be yours, my Lord."[35]

Contemplate

May I, dear God, enter fully into my life each moment and then let go, giving glory, honor, and blessing to you, who care so deeply for me. I praise and bless you, Lord, and I give thanks to you, and I will serve you in all humility. In union with all creation, at one with our source and Creator, I give thanks and praise in Eucharistic thanksgiving. Amen.

Imitate

Contemplate God's intimate presence in your life and heart. Contemplate Love's integral spirit giving life and breath to all living organisms. Spend time in the next days looking at God's creation and praising God for all the ways that you connect to and benefit from Brother Sun, Sister Moon, Brother Air, and Sister Earth.

---

35. Francis of Assisi, "The Canticle of Brother Sun," *Omnibus*, p. 131.

32 | JESUS TRULY PRESENT

Michelle Frazier, FSPA associate

Gaze

"And so it is really the spirit of God who dwells in his faithful who receive the most holy Body and Blood of our Lord."[36]

Consider

As Catholic Christians we believe that our Savior is truly present in the Eucharist. Each time we come before our God in adoration and prayer, we acknowledge the offering that Jesus gave us— his life, our liberation. We come before our God knowing that God is present before us and that God loves each one of us. Consider then, as we gaze upon the Blessed Sacrament, our belief in our Savior and the power of prayer. "Again, truly I tell you, if two of you agree on earth about anything you ask, it will be done for you by my Father in heaven" (Matthew 18:19). Prayer is not passive but active. When we pray, we allow ourselves to surrender and trust that God is with us in our hearts, present in the Eucharist and present in the world.

---

36. Francis of Assisi, "The Admonitions," *Omnibus,* p. 78.

Contemplate

O precious and beautiful Savior, I come before you this hour to adore and to worship you. Come fill my heart with your love. As you fill my heart with your love, allow that love to overflow out of me so that it may shine onto your children and onto all of your creation. I thank you, Jesus, for offering your life to all of humanity and to me. Thank you for your glory and for your mercy, and help me to be worthy to call you Brother and Savior. Amen.

Imitate

As you finish your prayer this day, take with you the belief that Jesus is truly present with us in the Eucharist. Because he is with us, let us imitate him by living our lives in humility, love, graciousness, tenderness, and charity toward all of our sisters and brothers.

33 | FEAR NO EVIL

Carl Koch, FSPA prayer partner

Gaze

"When the Saracens entered the cloister of the said monastery, the Lady made them bring her to the entrance of the refectory and bring a small box where there was the Blessed Sacrament of the Body of our Lord Jesus Christ. Throwing herself prostrate on the ground in prayer, she begged with tears, saying among other things: 'Lord, look upon these servants of yours, because I cannot protect them.' Then the witness [Sister Francesca] heard a voice of wonderful sweetness. 'I will always defend you!'"[37]

Consider

In 1244, Emperor Frederick II was at war with the pope. Frederick enlisted Muslims, or Saracens, as they were called then, to fight for him. When the Saracens attacked Assisi and San Damiano and its convent, St. Clare, who was ill and bedridden, had herself carried to the convent gate. She set there in sight of the enemy a wooden box containing the Eucharist and she prayed for her sisters' protection. Seeing Clare's courage and that of her sisters, the invaders withdrew from the convent.

---

37. "The Acts of the Process of Canonization of Clare of Assisi," *CA:ED,* p. 165.

The presence of Christ, who faced the terrors of the cross and rose from the grave, continues to protect those who believe that death cannot have the final word. Praying in the Holy Presence can strengthen us just as it did Clare and her sisters. Living the life of Christ, setting our hearts on being in peace and living in joy, protects us from the forces in our world that would strip us of our integrity and our care for others and lead us to violence and destruction. Praying in the Holy Presence reminds us that we need fear no evil. We are always in God's care. The Eucharist is a visible sign of God's loving-kindness and protection.

Contemplate

God of compassionate care, protect me from my fears, no matter the source. As with Clare, let my courage come from setting my heart on your way, your truth, your life. May I be a reminder that your world is actually filled with blessings. Then I will fear no evil. Amen. Alleluia.

Imitate

Offer your fears to God. With your eyes closed, sit comfortably with your hands, palms down, on your thighs. Bring to mind one fear at a time and hand each one over to your God of loving-kindness. Imagine each fear dropping out of your hands and into God's care.

34 | THE HIDDEN SWEETNESS OF GOD

Carl Koch, FSPA prayer partner

Gaze

"So that you too may feel what His friends feel
as they taste the hidden sweetness
that God Himself has reserved from the beginning
for those who love Him…
…totally love Him.

Who gave Himself totally for your love, …"[38]

Consider

The correspondence between Clare and Agnes of Prague, a Bohemian princess who had left royal life to become a Poor Clare, shows Clare's great heart and deep wisdom. All relationships require time to learn about one another, to appreciate each other's heart and soul. The tenderness and wisdom manifested in Clare's correspondence with Agnes illustrate Clare's commitment to take that time to nurture their relationship. Our relationship with the Divine One needs time too. Clare's loving counsel to Agnes remains sound eight hundred years later. In the presence of the Eucharist, we intentionally turn our attention to the Divine Lover. We take a "long loving look at the Real"—the ultimate, timeless God. And so we enter a space in which God's love for us can

---

38. Clare of Assisi, "The Third Letter to Agnes of Prague," *CA:ED,* pp. 45–46.

be manifest. Praying before the Divine Presence becomes one more way for us to offer our love to the one Lover who returns love totally. We pour out our needs, our faith, our thanks, and then we listen. God might not speak in fire or thunder. Rather, he speaks divine love mostly in a gentle breeze, as to Elijah on the mountain.

Contemplate

Divine Lover, your love is always present to me. I am the one who is absent. Too often I rush about doing this and that. I become disoriented, unfocused, and burnt out. Slow me down, Divine One, enough to spend time with you. Like Clare and Agnes, may we carve out space to renew our understanding and love for one another. You whisper loving-kindness to me; help me listen. You teach me how to live abundantly; help me embrace your wisdom. Come in. Come into my heart. Amen.

Imitate

The English word *spirit* comes from the Latin *spiritus,* meaning "breath." Breathing is life; God's spirit is lasting life. In harmony with your slow and deep breathing, pray to the Divine One: "I breathe out my fears, and breathe in your love" or "I breathe out my confusion, and breathe in your peace." Communicate today with someone you love and refresh your relationship. Be God's love for this person.

35 | THE FORCE FIELD OF LOVE

Karen Lueck, FSPA

Gaze

"Let us pray to God for one another,
   for by carrying each other's burden of charity in this way,
   we will easily fulfill the law of Christ [39]

Consider

Think of centripetal force. It is a powerful energy that acts as a magnet, drawing all to the source. The word *centripetal* means "to seek the center." When we come into the adoration chapel, we are being drawn by God, the ultimate Centripetal Force, to our center, to our true home.

But we are not the only one being drawn in; all of creation feels the pull. Science is telling us in many different ways that all life is connected on the most fundamental levels. This confirms what Christians have always believed—that we are one in Christ. And the bond of our unity is love.

So when we participate in the Eucharist and in adoration, we are not alone. Even though we may not see others, the force field of Christ's love is drawing all of us together. In receiving this love, we are transformed. We become love. And then the most natural thing to do is to manifest compassion

39. Clare of Assisi, "The Letter of St. Clare to Ermentrude of Bruges," *CA:ED,*
   p. 55.

outward. We pray for each other. We are present to each other. We carry each other's burdens joyfully.

As St. Clare says, in carrying each other's burdens, we fulfill the law of Christ. We enter the force field of love and compassion, the reign of God.

Contemplate

My Beloved, as you draw me to yourself this day, may I willingly enter your centripetal force of love. May I be transformed into love. May I be one with all the others you are also drawing to yourself, my brothers and sisters in creation: my human family, the bear and the turtle, the stars, the majestic trees, the smallest wildflower, the sun and the moon, the seas. May I feel the pain infecting your beautiful creation—famine, war, pollution, discrimination, disease. Help me to carry these burdens, knowing that love is healing and that you will continue to bring us all to you. Amen.

Imitate

As you leave your time of prayer, continue in your contemplative stance. Become aware that everyone you see is your brother or sister. Greet each as you pass by.

36 | PATH TO THE SACRED

Linda Mershon, FSPA

Gaze

"When I cannot attend Mass, I adore the Body of Christ with the eyes of the spirit in my prayer."[40]

Consider

The body of Christ, in the monstrance, on the altar or in the adoration chapel is where we give praise and glory to the God of All and where we petition the Beloved to tend to our deepest needs. The monstrance is a living symbol of the ways in which Christ manifests himself for us. Christ is the essence of all—of nature, ideas, relationships, energy. Whenever, wherever our hearts are moved to prayer, to supplication, to praise, glory, or adoration, we abide in the essence of Christ. Adoration is a state of being, and Christ's body—whether manifest in the monstrance, in the love between mother and child, or in the miracle of photosynthesis that creates oxygen—is an invitation and a path to the sacred.

---

40. Francis of Assisi, quoted by Br. Leo, "Thirteenth-Century Testimonies," *Omnibus,* p. 1607.

Contemplate

Beloved, give me the eyes, the mind, and the heart to see you and adore you as the essence of all. Allow that realization to make me fall down in adoration of you and all your creation. May my being, in a state of adoration at all times, be what opens our hearts to peace, within and throughout the world.

Imitate

Where are you at this moment? Look around you or go within and see your place in your mind's eye. Whatever or whoever you see, wherever you are, however you are, you abide in the essence of Christ, in adoration.

37 | MAKE A DWELLING PLACE

Marianna Ableidinger, FSPA

Gaze

"We should make a dwelling-place within ourselves where he can stay, he who is the Lord God almighty, Father, Son, and Holy Spirit."[41]

Consider

St. Francis was eager to repair the church of San Damiano. It was falling into ruins. He wanted to make for the Most High God a dwelling place where people could come to pray before the crucified Christ. Christ had spoken to him from the cross, saying, "Francis, do you not see that my house is falling to ruin? Go, and repair it for me."[42]

How many people there have been over the years who have worked to prepare for our Lord a suitable dwelling in their churches, from the simplest to the most elaborate! For St. Francis, it was not only buildings that provided a dwelling place in which to pray. He sought out caves among the mountains where he could find solitude to communicate intimately with Jesus.

In adoration of the Blessed Sacrament, we seek a place of quiet for a heart-to-heart talk with Jesus. We may also

---

41. Francis of Assisi, "The Rule of 1221," *Omnibus,* p. 49.
42. "Legend of the Three Companions," *Omnibus,* p. 903.

be seeking what a dwelling signifies: a home, a place of love, a place where family and friends share freely, a place of intimacy, a place of safety and security, and a place to find warmth, rest, and comfort. We believe that Jesus in his presence in the Blessed Sacrament wants to fulfill these desires to be at home.

Contemplate

Jesus, may I make of my heart a home where you may dwell. May you always find the door unlocked and open. May I eagerly await your entry day and night. Thank you for your presence in the Blessed Sacrament and in my heart. Amen.

Imitate

In your visit to a church or chapel for adoration, enter fully into the solitude and quiet of the dwelling place to meet God. Determine other places, if any, where you can make a dwelling place for God and be alone and quiet.

38 | HOLY DANCE OF THE TRINITY

Emily Dykman, FSPA affiliate

Gaze

"Moreover, she [Clare] especially spent day and night giving herself assiduously to vigils and prayers."[43]

Consider

As Francis knelt before the cross in the church of San Damiano and heard the voice of God speak to him, he knew his "yes" meant there would be no turning back. He needed to believe wholeheartedly in the mission to which God had called him. Like Francis, Clare offers us an example of commitment that is often difficult to practice. To commit oneself to something, to another, requires that one let go of one's own needs. One is required to think first of the other. Clare's consistent practice of prayer drew her into communion with God and with her community. God's own being is one of relationship, and we are reminded that we enter into this holy dance of the Trinity when we enter into prayer and contemplation. Our prayer draws us into deeper communion with God and into stronger commitment to the common good.

---

43. Alexander IV, "The Papal Bull of the Canonization of Clare," *CA:ED*, p. 243.

Contemplate

Gracious and loving God, in your presence I am reminded of your call to me to be in relationship with you and with the entirety of your creation. My prayer is to be drawn closer to you in my contemplation and in my interactions with your beautiful world. May I commit myself to a life rooted in prayer so that my presence in the world is one of peace, compassion, and reverence. May I truly be your image and presence in the world. Amen.

Imitate

Throughout your work today, consider how your prayer has rooted you and how that prayer extends you into communion with God and those with whom you interact. How have you extended a prayerful presence into the world through both your words and your actions? How do you respond to God's invitation to join the holy dance of the Trinity?

39 | PUT ON CHRIST

Carl Koch, FSPA prayer partner

Gaze

"Finally, while receiving the Lord's Body and Blood,
she [Clare] sheds burning tears, and not only fears and
    honors Christ
hiding under the form of bread,
but venerates Him ruling heaven and earth."[44]

Consider

Receive can mean to acquire, to act as a receptacle, to assimilate through mind and senses, or to welcome. So when Clare, the devout lover of Christ, received the Eucharist, she truly welcomed the Christ, became a receptacle for Christ's love, and assimilated Christ. As St. Paul said, she "put on Christ." The moment transported her to intense veneration. Heightening the intensity of Eucharistic reception was the fact that in Clare's day reverencing the Eucharist was much more common than actually receiving Christ's body and blood. Indeed, most Christians received the Eucharist only once a year. Adding to the mystery and special power of the Eucharist, altars in medieval churches were built further away from the assembly and were virtually hidden behind

44. "The Versified Legend of the Virgin Clare," *CA:ED,* p. 211.

ornate screens. No wonder Clare shed tears of joy when receiving, welcoming, assimilating her Divine Lover.

Contemplate

Holy One, Savior, Light of lights, truly God, welcome. Reside in my heart to warm my affections. Live in my mind to teach me your wisdom. Abide in my will to give me courage in the face of hard decisions. May I receive you as did Clare, with joy, hope, thankfulness, and celebration. Amen.

Imitate

The great theologian Thomas Aquinas, Clare's contemporary, wrote the famous hymn "Tantum Ergo" to celebrate the Eucharist. Sing or pray its words or those of any Eucharistic hymn and then offer thanksgiving for all the ways in which Christ has transformed your life to be fuller, livelier, and more loving.

40 | CONSTANT GRATITUDE

Marci Madary, FSPA affiliate

Gaze

"At all times and seasons, in every country and place, every day and all day, we must have a true and humble faith, and keep him in our hearts, where we must love, honour, adore, serve, praise and bless, glorify and acclaim, magnify and thank, the most high supreme and eternal God."[45]

Consider

Francis walked on this earth with a constant song of praise on his lips. He never tired of seeking union with the Creator and easily fell into deep and sustained prayer. And the depth of his love for the Incarnate God drew people to him, in his lifetime and still today. While Francis appeared to do this effortlessly, keeping our relationship with God fresh and alive can be a challenge. Even if we begin a prayer practice with much enthusiasm, our zeal can wane. Soon our prayer time can become mundane and leave an aftertaste. Our minds wander, our bodies go through the motions, and our words become rote. Looking at Francis' life, we can see that his constant gratitude for God's goodness gave his prayer life

---

45. Francis of Assisi, "The Rule of 1221," *Omnibus,* p. 52.

vitality. Likewise, by turning our hearts to thanksgiving and acknowledging God's blessings in our lives, we can infuse our prayer with energy. We can experience renewal.

Contemplate

Loving God, help my prayer life to remain fresh and full of life. Your blessings are abundant. Open my eyes to the many ways you are present in this world. Give me the grace to perceive small miracles that surround me. May I recognize your beauty and goodness in every moment, in every breath. Like my brother Francis, may my lips be filled with praise and thanksgiving. Give me a heart filled with gratitude that my prayer be ever renewed. Amen.

Imitate

How has your prayer grown stale? Acknowledge it and consider how you can revitalize your prayer practice. Begin each prayer time by thanking God for five blessings in your life. Do not repeat blessings but continually find new gifts from the Creator. Allow the praise on your lips to infuse your prayer time.

41 | IN ALL GOD'S CHURCHES

Anita Beskar, FSPA

Gaze

"We adore you, Lord Jesus Christ, here and in all your churches in the whole world, and we bless you, because by your holy cross you have redeemed the world."[46]

Consider

Visiting churches seems to be a popular component of many tourist experiences, especially in Europe. The beauty of the windows, the grandeur of the architecture, and the enduring wonder of the frescoes capture our imagination. Often, in the midst of this ancient art we are called back, through the presence of a small burning candle, to the source of this grandeur, the Eucharistic Presence. If, in our explorations, we are privileged to join a worshiping community celebrating the Mass, we have an added experience of church. As we join the worshiping community, we recall that church is more than a building. It is a community of believers that in its unity crosses continents and cultures.

Many years ago in the open plains of central Iowa, Pope John Paul II celebrated Eucharist amid the blustery winds of an October day. The pope's presence in itself was a symbol

---

46. Francis of Assisi, "The Testament of St. Francis," *Omnibus,* p. 67.

of unity. But it was in the recitation of the Creed by the thousands gathered that this unity was proclaimed loud and clear.

Are buildings and gatherings of believers the only experiences of what we call "church"? Does not the beauty of a sunrise or the silence of a secluded woodland provide an experience of the presence of the goodness and grandeur of God? Cannot the whole of the universe in its mystery and wonder become for us "church" in which we are invited to adore the Source and Sustainer of all Creation?

Contemplate

Jesus, I adore you in the church in which I now find myself. Open my eyes to see your presence throughout my day. Slow me down so that I do not move from one experience to another in frenzy. In this way make my day an experience of adoration. Amen.

Imitate

Take time to "see" God's presence in the "church" of your experiences. Adore God in the beauty of a flower, experience the presence of God's Spirit in the movement of the wind, and listen to God's voice in an encounter with a family member, neighbor, or coworker.

42 | THE COURAGE TO BE RECONCILED

Anita Beskar, FSPA

Gaze

"I beg you to show the greatest possible reverence and honour for the most holy Body and Blood of our Lord Jesus Christ through whom *all things, whether on the earth or in the heavens,* have been brought to peace and reconciled with the Almighty God." [47]

Consider

Our world yearns for peace. Yet terror, violence, and broken relationships seem to be in the very air we breathe. This toxic air seems to poison our deepest spirits as we open ourselves to receive peace.

Francis, too, experienced the allurement of war. But in the midst of its seeming glory, God "stopped him short"—not in a clear voice but in pain, disillusionment, and fear. To Francis' surprise it was in this very confusion that he heard the voice of God in new questions that he wrestled with.

We, too, wrestle in our desire for peace. In the utter confusion we experience around us, it is easy to place the burden of reconciliation and peacemaking in the hands of others. But deep within we know that true peace can

---

47. Francis of Assisi, "Letter to a General Chapter," *Omnibus,* p. 104.

emerge only as each one of us reconciles his or her broken relationships. We, like Francis, are invited to enter the depths of our inner being and find there the Real Presence of Divine Good, the source of peace. In this Real Presence we find our courage to be reconciled.

Contemplate

Spirit of the living God, as I breathe in your presence, I open myself to my deep yearning for peace. Fill me with gratitude for the peace that already is your gift. Give me the courage to probe the crevices of my heart that are cluttered with the residue of resentment, anger, and judgments that block me from more fully receiving your gift of peace. Strengthen my desire to surrender these blocks to your healing mercy so that I may be peace today. Amen.

Imitate

Carry the gift of God's reconciling presence into your day, becoming aware of at least one person in whom you sense a lack of peace. Through a smile, a comforting word, or an act of thoughtfulness, may you become Eucharistic presence. In this small act you join peacemakers across our world in a shared effort to become reconciled to the all-powerful God.

43 | GOD'S LOVE POURED OUT

Darlene Wozney, FSPA affiliate

Gaze

"They are truly peacemakers who are able to preserve their peace of mind and heart for the love of our Lord Jesus Christ, despite all that they suffer in this world."[48]

Consider

We come to prayer with all the pain and trauma we have suffered in our lives. As we sit with other adorers, we realize it is so quiet that we can "hear" the quiet. We can also hear Jesus telling us he loves us. He gives us peace. He gives us joy. He gives us hope. He gives us the grace of forgiveness, to forgive and be forgiven, to be filled with peace. As Psalm 23 reminds us, "Surely goodness and mercy shall follow me all the days of my life." We receive encouragement in our suffering from St. Paul in his letter to the Romans (5:3–6) when he invites us to boast of our afflictions. His message is challenging, but he assures us that affliction makes for endurance, for tested virtue, and for hope. He tells us that hope will not leave us disappointed because the love of God has been poured out in our hearts through the Holy Spirit, who has been given to us.

---

48. Francis of Assisi, "The Admonitions," *Omnibus,* p. 83.

Contemplate

Loving, gracious, gentle Jesus, hear my hope-filled prayer. Fill me with joy, a joy that bubbles out of me onto all I meet this day. May the peace I feel grow as large as your presence. Amen.

Imitate

As you leave this sacred space filled with joy and peace, invite the whole world to see Jesus in you. See Jesus in each person you meet.

44 | EVERY MOMENT THINE

Kathleen Kenkel, FSPA

Gaze

"O Sacrament most holy, O Sacrament divine,
All praise and all thanksgiving be every moment thine."[49]

Consider

Franciscan Sisters of Perpetual Adoration have prayed this prayer in our adoration chapel every hour, day and night, for over 133 years. This fulfillment of a promise has been espoused as our charism and as the ministry of our St. Rose Convent Community in La Crosse, Wisconsin. It is our privilege and our joy. Our splendid adoration chapel is filled with beautiful angels in every artistic form. We almost hear their "Glory to God…" echoing as we enter. A great quiet and a fullness of peace descend on all who enter. We bow reverently. Our eyes focus on Christ in the Eucharistic host. Like a magnet, we are drawn into this Holy of Holies. We surrender to the sacred mystery, which engulfs us.

---

49. FSPA archives, "Daily Devotions—Morning Devotions" (undated).

Contemplate

Lord, I hear a voice saying, "Be with me." Christ and my inner Spirit are one. In silence, I commune with you, Christ Jesus, my brother, my friend, my spouse. I pray for all in our Church, our world, our country, our city; for our Franciscan Sisters of Perpetual Adoration, family, and friends; for all who are suffering and all who are in need. Amen.

Imitate

Share the fruits of your adoration experience with those you meet. Like St. Francis, pause and invite all to join you in praising God in all creation and in rejoicing in the beauty of all that our wondrous God has made.

45 | SHARE JESUS' PRESENCE

Bernice Newton, FSPA

Gaze

"May the Lord always be with you and may you always be with Him. Amen."[50]

Consider

How privileged we are to have the precious gift of the Blessed Sacrament! In the early beginnings of our religious community in Milwaukee, the sisters felt the deep need to have Jesus present in our chapel. In the life of St. Francis, we learn that he spent entire nights on Mt. Alverno in solitary prayer. St. Clare of Assisi was noted for her deep devotion to the Blessed Sacrament. Her blessing shows how she encouraged her sisters to be aware of Jesus' presence in their personal lives. There is a growing need for quiet and prayerful times, as we exist in such a complex world with so many distractions. Jesus' personal living presence to each person is so much needed.

---

50. Clare of Assisi, "The Blessing of Clare of Assisi," *CA:ED,* p. 82.

Contemplate

Jesus, I am thankful to have this time of adoration. Teach me how to share your loving presence with all those around me, especially those who are suffering and feel not only physical pain but confusion. Father, Jesus, Spirit, I adore you, I lay my life before you, I love you. Amen.

Imitate

Pray the "Peace Prayer" attributed to St. Francis: "Make me an instrument of your peace. Where there is hatred, let me sow love; Where there is injury, pardon; and Where there is doubt, true faith in you." Try to bring this message to everyone who crosses your path today.

46 | FULLY HUMAN IN LOVE

Kathy Roberg, FSPA

Gaze

"For the Lord Himself has placed us not only as a form for others in being an example and mirror, but even for our sisters whom the Lord has called to our way of life as well, that they in turn might be a mirror and example to those living in the world."[51]

Consider

We are all born in the image and likeness of God. We are created to be real, to live in and out of our true identity in God, thereby being true reflections of God. If we gaze on Christ—who he was in history and still is in our present world—and truly see how he reached out in unconditional love and in compassion in service to others, do we then see our own loving actions and service reflecting Christ's image? Do we see as in a mirror Christ's reflection on and in us and our actions? We are present with the living God in the totality of our lives. We look into others' eyes that yearn for acceptance. We pass lost souls on our journey. Sometimes we avoid getting entangled in the mixed-up spiral of others' lives. We hear the cry of the poor on our streets. But do we?

---

51. Francis of Assisi, "The Testament," *CA:ED*, p. 57.

Do we allow ourselves to be touched by hearts that ache for love? Do we allow ourselves to be fully human in service of love for others?

Contemplate

Jesus, you allowed yourself to be fully human. You faced your fears of rejection, doubt, being ostracized, and yet you touched others' hearts in service. You let your heart beat with others and the eyes of your soul to see into the depths of others' pains and needs. I know you created me for a purpose. I am mysteriously driven to go out of myself. I ache to truly listen to the pain and cries of the poor. Yet I hold back at times, not knowing the consequences of being human. Help me to trust. Place my hand in yours. Let your feet guide me as I strive to live as you did and as you would want me to. Amen.

Imitate

Stepping out of this sacred space may be scary. Trust in God's constant love and support. Let your eyes smile, see beyond appearances, into aching souls. Let your heart touch and beat with other hearts and help them feel accepted. Reach out and be the hands and heart of Christ's love in service to others. Help make Christ present today.

47 | THE GAZE THAT NEVER WAVERS

Barb Kruse, FSPA prayer partner

Gaze

"You are holy, Lord, the only God,
  and your deeds are wonderful."[52]

Consider

Francis entered into life each day exploding with love and reverence for all of creation. He was fully aware of God's goodness permeating every aspect of life. Like a young child tenderly gazing into the eyes of his mother, with a heart full of unconditional love, Francis, too, gazes at the Eucharist, at the leper, at the sultan, at the sun and the moon and his brothers and sisters—with humility, awe, and love. We are also invited into that same awareness of the goodness of God permeating our lives. A beautiful sunset, a warm bed to sleep in, restored health, job security, a meal on the table.

---

52. Francis of Assisi, "Praises of God," *Omnibus,* p. 125.

Contemplate

Lord, I know you love me. I know that you look constantly at me with an unwavering love and wonder that holds no bounds. Yet I continue to turn away, distracted by the noise of life around me, by my inner voice that whispers of my unworthiness, by my own brokenness. Help me to trust in my goodness, to accept with wonder and amazement that gaze that never wavers. Amen.

Imitate

Look around you. How is God's goodness revealed to you this day? What do you pay attention to? Where do you fix your gaze? Recall times when you were gently reminded of God's unwavering love for you. How did you respond? What grace do you seek this day to help you respond more fully to this promise of unconditional love and acceptance?

48 | CONSCIOUSLY INVITE LOVE

Lucy Slinger, FSPA

Gaze

"Do not be afraid, daughter.
  God, Who is faithful in all His words
    and holy in all His deeds,
  will pour His blessings upon you and your sisters."[53]

Consider

Blessed is the one who believes in a God of love. Jesus used the phrase "do not fear" many times. Psychologists tell us love and fear cannot coexist. Francis of Assisi says, "Where there is Love and Wisdom, / there is neither Fear nor Ignorance. / Where there is Patience and Humility, / there is neither Anger nor Annoyance. / Where there is the Fear of God to guard the dwelling, / there no enemy can enter. / Where there is Mercy and Prudence / there is neither Excess nor Harshness."[54] These are paradoxical thoughts, which embrace "fear" as knowledge of a God of love, a God who blesses one with protection and gives abundance in life. If one truly believes that "God is love," then there is absolutely no need for a fearful heart, even in the most challenging times in life.

---

53. Clare of Assisi, "The Letter of St. Clare to Ermentrude of Bruges," *CA:ED*, p. 55.
54. Francis of Assisi, "The Admonitions," *Omnibus,* p. 86.

Contemplate

Creator who made all out of your infinite, unconditional love, Word made Flesh, who showed me how to unconditionally love in life, and Spirit ever present within me and all of creation, crack open the fears that remain in my heart. Let me grow in knowing your loving presence in every event of the day. Let me feel the abundance of your love with gratitude in all the actions I take this and every day. Save me from fear, anger, worry, self-pity, or foolish decisions that harden my heart so that your love in me and with me is a conscious part of every moment of my day. Amen.

Imitate

Do your actions imitate Jesus' call to love the Divine, yourself, and every aspect of creation? Little actions like choosing a cloth napkin over a paper napkin or using scrap paper to write a grocery list or greeting others out of genuine love show reverence and respect for creation. List ways you can consciously invite love to trump fear in your life.

49 | RESPECT AND REVERENCE ALL CREATION

Kathy Roberg, FSPA

Gaze

"I beg you to show the greatest possible reverence and honour for the most holy Body and Blood of our Lord Jesus Christ, through whom *all things, whether on the earth or in the heavens,* have been brought to peace and reconciled with Almighty God."[55]

Consider

The body and blood of our Lord Jesus Christ present in the Eucharist is also the people who make up the Body of Christ. I implore all of you—I beg you—to show respect, reverence, honor for this body and blood. God begs us to show respect for his creation! Why should God have to beg us to respect his own body and blood—God's creation? We should be honored to do this! We are all a part of this Body. Do we not respect and care for our own bodies? Our world is so filled with violence and disrespect for life in general. We see it on TV and in advertisements. We see it on our streets. This disregard for life, we see it with respect to Mother Earth. We see it even in the confused and turbulent skies that cover our world. St. Francis pleaded with the entire Franciscan Order, and pleads as well with us, the entire world, to respect, to

---

55. Francis of Assisi, "Letter to a General Chapter," *Omnibus,* p. 104.

reverence life, the body and blood of our Lord. We fully believe in the presence of God here, God's body and blood. We, who especially live out of Franciscan values, have the power to bring about a change and give the reverence and honor due to this body and blood of our Lord.

Contemplate

O God, you are the source of all life, life in your body and blood. You are totally present in the Eucharist, which nourishes and unites us, and in all of creation—people, humanity, nature, events, situations—all that makes up life. I look around and see the wonders and wondrous beauty, the mystery of life. How can I not give praise, honor, and respect? You have placed me in your midst. I stand in awe of you, O God. Help me to walk gently with life, to care for this gift that is so generously, constantly given. I have only this one life to live, to respect and praise. I will take ownership and begin this quest today. Amen.

Imitate

Cherish the quiet, protected space and time of prayer for which you have just let your mind and heart go to another world. As you step forth into the real world with its pains and disruptions, stop, smell the air, let the breeze flow over you, and open your eyes to the awe of all life. Respect, reverence, adore, and give praise for the body and blood of our Lord. God is present in all.

50 | LOOK UPON CHRIST CRUCIFIED

Joan Weisenbeck, FSPA

Gaze

"Look upon Him [the poor Christ] who became contemptible
for you,

and follow Him, making yourself contemptible in this
world for Him."[56]

Consider

Clare modeled her life on the humanity of Jesus. By gazing
upon the image of the crucified Christ, she came to identify
with his poverty. Her vision of poverty had a privileged place
in her life, because Jesus is the Poor Crucified. Because of
her encounter with the crucified Christ, she could witness to
the world what intimacy with Christ really is. She found her
spiritual understanding of love in gazing on the visual image
of the crucified Christ. For Clare to gaze daily upon the face
of the crucified is the way to spiritual transformation, because
Christ is the invisible God made visible. Clare encouraged
daily prayer before the cross, something every person can
do. To contemplate Christ crucified is to look at ourselves
and others and know that death does not have the last word
because Jesus, risen in glory, speaks the Word of Life, given
to us in the Scriptures.

---

56. Clare of Assisi, "The Second Letter to Agnes of Prague," *CA:ED*, p. 42.

Contemplate

O God, like Clare, I gaze upon the crucified Christ, to become like the one I see. As I contemplate Jesus I see myself with new eyes as I look at him looking back at me with love and delight. I imagine the feelings that Jesus has for me as he gazes upon me in love, and I am silent and rest in this awareness. Amen.

Imitate

Like Clare, choose wisely who or what you look upon. What do you gaze upon in your daily experience of life and when you come to prayer? Do you experience yourself as beloved by God, both flawed and graced? Imitate this Jesus of the Gospels, and follow his way by living out the limits of love.

51 | PROBE FOR INNER WISDOM

Linda Kerrigan, FSPA affiliate

Gaze

"[She]… continually occupying her soul
with sacred prayers and divine praises.
She had already focused
the most fervent attention of her entire desire
on the Light
and
she opened more generously the depths of her mind
to the torrents of grace
that bathe a world of turbulent change."[57]

Consider

We are told that in the beginning there was light. Ever since, all of God's creation—plants, animals, we humans—are drawn to light. As we emerged from our mothers' wombs and pushed our way through a dark and confining birth canal, we experienced light for the very first time. We have come to learn how light sustains us and calls us to life. We call Jesus "Light of the World," and he invites us to be light for one another in ways of loving, caring, and serving. Without this light, ours would be a dark, fearful, oppressive journey.

---

57. "The Legend of St. Clare," *CA:ED*, pp. 273–274.

Our time spent in adoration gifts us with light in multiple forms: glowing candles, daylight streaming through stained-glass windows, the lit-up faces of other prayerful adorers, the pearl-like divine shine of the Blessed Sacrament.

Contemplate

God of light and love, you draw me near, holding me as a fragile and precious infant. Light my way as I joyfully follow you on the path traveled before me by Sister Clare and Brother Francis. Their modeled lives of faith and fidelity shed light on how and where I take my next step. May I walk boldly, confidently, and reverently as we are stirred to do what is ours to do. Amen.

Imitate

Move from contemplation to action and probe for inner wisdom. What kind of light do others see in you? Do you have enough light to see your way? How do you fill the oil in your lamp? Who needs you today to bring a bit of sunshine into their life? As you generously share your light, give thanks and praise in knowing and treasuring all that is gift.

52 | RIGHT RELATIONSHIP WITH GOD

Amy Taylor, FSPA

Gaze

"May you do well in the Lord, as I hope I myself do. And remember me and my sisters in your prayers."[58]

Consider

We follow many things in our lives. We follow road maps, instructions, street signs, rules, and even advice from others. When we follow the call of God to discipleship, we choose to give our lives in service to something that is greater than ourselves. St. Clare encourages us to follow God in a way that is in keeping with the example of our Lord Jesus Christ. To follow, we must let go of all that keeps us from being the best of who we were created to be. To follow we must listen. As we gaze on the Blessed Sacrament, we are reminded that discipleship calls us into right relationship with our God, and with one another.

Contemplate

God, help me to see you in every moment of my life. May I see in the model of your Son Jesus how following you changes my life and opens my eyes to the world around

---

58. Clare of Assisi, "The Third Letter to Agnes of Prague," *CA:ED,* p. 48.

me. May my awareness of you continue to grow as I seek these quiet moments in my day. Guide me on this path of discipleship and be with me in every step I take. To follow I must take time to listen. Amen.

Imitate

As you move through your day, become aware of how every moment is a prayer to God. Look anew at the environment that you live in. How can you offer a model of contemplation in the midst of the busyness of everyday life? Jesus continually took quiet time and moments in the midst of ministry to strengthen his relationship with God. He also blessed, praised, and openly called on God and the Holy Spirit to intervene and help those he walked among. How can you follow in his footsteps and pray for those whom you encounter?

BIBLIOGRAPHY

Clare of Assisi. *Clare of Assisi: Early Documents.* Edited and translated by Regis J. Armstrong. St. Bonaventure, N.Y.: Franciscan Institute, 1993.

Forbes, Francis Alice. *Life of Pius X.* London: Burns, Oates and Washbourne, 1918.

Francis of Assisi. *Francis of Assisi: Early Documents.* Vol. 1. Edited by Regis J. Armstrong, J.A. Wayne Hellmann, and William Short. New York: New City, 1999.

———. *St. Francis of Assisi: Writings and Early Biographies: English Omnibus of the Sources for the Life of St. Francis.* Edited by Marion A. Habig. Cincinnati: St. Anthony Messenger Press, 2008.

FSPA archives. "Daily Devotions—Morning Devotions." Undated.

Margaret Mary Alacoque. Letter to John Croiset, s.j. (November 2, 1689). In *The Letters of St. Margaret Mary Alaocque,* edited by Clarence A. Herbst. Charlotte, N.C.: TAN, 2009.